INFLUENCING
COMMUNICATION

INFLUENCING COMMUNICATION
A Practioner's Guide To Internal Communication Consultancy

LIZ COCHRANE

THE INDUSTRIAL SOCIETY

First published 1997 by
The Industrial Society
48 Bryanston Square
London W1H 7LN
Tel. 0171 262 2401

ISBN 1 85835 488 9

Typeset by: GCS
Printed by: Optichrome
Cover Design: Form Graphic Design

The Industrial Society is a Registered Charity No. 290003

contents

foreword and acknowledge-ments

This book has been written as a result of the help of a large number of communication professionals who were kind enough to spare me their time in the Spring and early Summer of 1996. Originally I had embarked on a project to gather examples of "live" documentation used by practitioners who are acting as internal consultants to their organisations. It soon became apparent that the real value of this exercise was not simply the documents, but the advice, hints and tips which formed the stories behind the pieces of paper.

This paperback is a collation of that advice, illustrated by mini case studies of strategies that had been employed prior to my research. In some cases, the comments made are clearly attributed to one individual. But as many of the themes that developed were reiterated by a number of the professionals I spoke to, I have amalgamated the majority of comments for ease of reading. However, all that follows is thanks to the generosity of the people I interviewed in sharing their experiences and learning. A separate and larger manual combines their advice with examples of the documents used in organisations.

Thanks are also due to the following, for providing me with contact names and with ideas for the bibliography: Eileen Scholes of the ITEM Group plc; Andraea Dawson-Shepherd of Hedron Consulting Ltd; Andrew Lambert of People in Business; Colette Dorward of Smythe Dorward Lambert; Jenny Davenport and Paul Davis of the

Industrial Society, and Richard Varey of the BNFL Corporate Communications Unit at Salford University. From these individuals I gathered more leads than I could possibly follow through in the time available — testimony to the quality of work currently underway in the world of internal communication.

May I also thank my colleagues on the advisory group of the Employee Communications Association for their help and support, with special mentions for Dominic Walters of Austin Knight for penning the chapter on "Getting the most from external consultants" and Teresa Ford of BT for painstakingly reading through and commenting on the final proofs. Finally, thanks to the management of Glaxo Wellcome Operations for their help and support while I was researching the book.

the organisations

Influencing communication is based on the real life experience of communication practitioners and managers, who have shared the approach they have taken to effective internal communication in their organisations. This book distills their advice and comments. It does not therefore necessarily contain specific references to every organisation listed below.

Automobile Association – *Phillipa Stokes*
Arthur Andersen Consulting – *Craig Smith*
BT – *Teresa Ford*
Bass Taverns – *Anna Foster*
BBC – *Alaric Mostyn*
BNFL Fuel Division – *Peter Osborne*
Boots – *Nicholas Wright*
The Body Shop – *James Harkness*
Cable and Wireless Business Networks – *Jane Mullins*
Cellnet – *Jennifer Johnson*
Digital – *Susan Robbie*
Glaxo Wellcome Operations – *Liz Cochrane*
ICL – *Laura Ferguson*
Inland Revenue – *Nicola Walters*
Lloyds Bank – *Paul Rudd*
Lombard Personal Finance – *Sarah Fasey*
London Borough of Redbridge – *Paul Williams*
The Tetley Group – *Debbie Standish*
National Grid Company – *Trevor Seeley*

National and Provincial Building Society – *Paul Chapman*
Nynex – *Adrian Seward*
Parcelforce – *John Payne*
Post Office Counters – *Harry James*
Royal Mail (Anglia) – *John Newson and team*
Royal Bank of Scotland – *Peter Casebow*
Unipart Group of Companies – *Frank Nigriello*

introduction

- This book has been compiled following a series of interviews with managers across a wide range of organisations who are responsible for employee communication. It aims to provide practical examples of the approach they have taken to being effective internal consultants and moving internal communication forward in their companies.

- Internal communication is a relatively new discipline. In 1995, Clutterbuck Associates & Business Intelligence Ltd studied the current state of play in the way internal communication is supporting organisational change. The "Is anyone listening?" survey was carried out across major UK organisations. Of 248 responses by self identified internal communication practitioners, only 22% said that their function had existed for more than five years.

- A survey of employee communication by the Industrial Society in 1994 as part of the Managing Best Practice series identified that 55% of the 915 organisations who responded employed someone with specific responsibility for employee communication. Of these, just under two thirds worked within personnel with 15% reporting direct to the chief executive. 14% were part of corporate communications or PR. At that time, only 29% of respondents had written communication policies, and just one in three linked employee communication to the company's strategic plan.

- However, as the importance of effective internal communication to support change and the achievement of business goals grows, so the role of the internal communication practitioner is changing. Rather than simply writing the internal staff newspaper, or managing the mechanics of the team briefing process, the internal communication person is increasingly being called on to be an internal consultant, providing advice and guidance to the organisation and a strategic approach to communication that directly supports business objectives. This book looks at four key areas which are vital for success in this internal consultancy role:
  — developing relationships with customers
  — identifying customer needs
  — developing communication strategies and plans
  — evaluating effectiveness
  suggestions are also made on the effective use of external consultants.

- As the nature of the job market changes, so people are becoming personally responsible for their development and their careers. We no longer rely on the organisation we are employed by to take career decisions on our behalf. Research by Andrew Lambert of People in Business indicated that a significant proportion of internal communication practitioners see the job as a temporary staging post in their careers. This means it is increasingly important for the internal communication person to manage their role in a way which develops robust communications in their company, while also increasing their personal experience and developing general managerial skills which will be useful in their future career. These skills could include strategy development; project managing a plan from conception to implementation; and monitoring and evaluating success.

- IMPORTANT HEALTH WARNING. Every organisation is unique. A strategy, plan — or even an approach — which has worked in one company at a particular time cannot simply be reproduced in another in order to achieve the same results. Every solution must be tailored to the needs and culture of the specific organisation. However, when approaching a new task it is valuable to gain an insight into what different organisations have done — and more fundamentally, how they did it.

1 developing customer relationships

The internal communication professional can only have a positive impact in their organisation by working through others. Success depends on:
— taking time to understand the demands facing the organisation and individual managers, then demonstrating how you can help achieve business objectives
— adding value at both a tactical and a strategic level
— learning to challenge effectively
— having clear definitions for the role of the internal communication practitioner and line managers, and ensuring that appropriate processes are in place to support managers as the key communicators in a business.

Qualities of the internal communication practitioner

- Frank Nigriello, Group Communications Director of Unipart describes the role of the internal communication practitioner as both an advisor and implementor.
  - Advisor: because the internal communicator should **challenge** accepted wisdom, and ensure that situations are seen from different perspectives, and in the widest possible **context**.

— Implementor: because the communicator's professional skills should provide a workable **solution** to the most intractable communication problem.

- So what kind of qualities does the internal communication consultant need in order to add value to their organisation? Contributors to the book thought the following important:
  — personal integrity
  — networking and developing strong relationships
  — challenging effectively
  — tenacity
  — assertiveness
  — hunger for information: internal and external
  — assimilation, interpretation and analysis of information
  — seeing the wider picture — so that messages can be put in context
  — promoting a range of viewpoints
  — presenting cases coherently to senior management
  — professionalism and expertise
  — not being a glory seeker: ensuring that others "own" the ideas.

Developing credibility

- The internal communicator needs a high level of credibility to be able to challenge, and to have advice and suggestions accepted. How can this be achieved?

- Some organisations select their internal communication champion by identifying a line manager who is already highly credible having delivered results in another part of the organisation. The manager of the "Understanding Process" in the National and Provincial Building Society (now merged with Abbey National) was recruited this way because her key task was to challenge the "Direction Team" whenever she thought that they were acting in conflict with what the company was trying to achieve.

- Get the support of the Chief Executive Officer or equivalent. Spend time exploring how your skills can help him/her achieve his/her objectives. Some practitioners develop a personal communication plan with him/her, ensuring that the plan is linked to the organisation's business objectives and that the messages to the various audiences inside and outside the organisation are clear and aligned. Once you have the commitment and backing of the CEO, you can begin to work with other managers.

- If you are not immersed in up-to-date business knowledge of your organisation, take time out to understand the demands facing your managers and people and the objectives they must meet. Go on the road with sales reps: spend time on the production line; join your purchasing people in meetings with suppliers. Do it on a regular basis. Become a generalist in your approach to business, rather than a specialist. This ensures you understand the needs and the constraints of your customers so you can add value to the business by challenging in an appropriate way and giving advice that will help your customers achieve their objectives.

- Find time to meet with key people in the business. Listen to them. Understand their needs, and the needs they perceive the organisation to have. Make sure that you understand:
  — their role
  — where they fit in the organisation
  — what they are contributing to the business
  — what they see as their communication needs/how you can support them.

- Avoid esoteric, theoretical discussions with customers. Use the opportunity of solving practical problems both to build your credibility and to increase people's understanding of effective communication. Make sure that you are available to customers when they need your help.

- Develop a relationship with customers that extends beyond work issues. Take time to ask them about their home life. One communication manager keeps an aide memoire in the shape of an organisational chart on which she notes key details about customers, their children's names, where they are going on holiday, etc. Another makes a policy of seeing people outside work time — discussing issues over dinner in a less formal environment.

- Don't spend your time exclusively with managers. If you are genuinely going to represent a range of perspectives, you need to understand what those perspectives are. Rather than relying exclusively on the results of surveys and other measurement tools to base your understanding of what is important to the people throughout your organisation, find opportunities to talk with them. Build in their needs and perspectives to the communication strategy.

- If you aim to be perceived as an advisor rather than a doer — find an area where you can offer immediate advice to a key customer to demonstrate your judgement — but don't offer to implement the solution on their behalf. Pass the responsibility for making it happen back to the appropriate line manager.

- Demonstrate by the questions you ask and comments you make that you are focused exclusively on your customer and their needs. Understand their perspective. Work through their problem with them. Help them identify how they can solve it.

- Avoid taking the credit for an effective solution. Ensure others "own" ideas and projects. Remember — you are the kingmaker not the king!

- Find opportunities for "quick wins" to build credibility and to demonstrate the contribution you can make to the business. Identify an immediate need that will help your customer achieve their objectives — then provide the solution. This could be as simple as planning and implementing a series of CEO letters for an organisation that lacks any communication on business direction from the top. The important factor is that the solution provides tangible, measurable, business improvements.

- Having won credibility through delivering results — or preferably in tandem with doing so — work on the long term strategy for communication. But avoid focusing exclusively on the long term without delivering immediate results. Most organisations aren't that patient. They want to see an immediate return on their investment in you!

Within six weeks of joining the organisation, Craig Smith, head of internal communication for Andersen Consulting, a worldwide firm of management consultants, converted the in-house journal from print to an electronic version run on Lotus Notes. Advantages included:
— the ability to "customise" the newsletter — targeting relevant information at specific audiences
— the opportunity for readers to call up additional background information and access business data relating to the story on their screens
— substantial cost savings
— the ability to monitor the profile of readership of articles by grade, country and organisational group.

- Don't bite off more than you can chew. Be clear on who your key customers are. Focus on providing them with an excellent service. Make sure you can stay close to them and understand their business needs. Several companies reported that they have recently restructured to have a small communication unit at the centre, plus people with a responsibility for communication in each operating division. This allows the local people to be close to their customers and understand their needs.

- Business crisis is often the time when communication comes into the sharpest focus. A number of communication practitioners commented that their profile had increased significantly during a time when the business faced its most significant risks. Using your specialist knowledge to recommend how best to communicate raises your profile and credibility. Two companies interviewed commented that following such circumstances, the role of communication has been enhanced and is now seen as an integral part of the company's management process. Members of the communication team now regularly attend and play a full role in meetings of the company's "top team" and are part of key project teams.

- Make sure you pay sufficient attention to the deliverables and to getting the simple things right. You may be a brilliant strategist, but if a name is spelt wrong in a newsletter, or a helpline number is not answered, your credibility will suffer.

- Building relationships is a bit like painting the Forth Bridge — a never-ending task. If a key customer leaves and is replaced — you need to do it all over again.

Challenging effectively/avoiding conflict

- A key role for the communication practitioner is to challenge the thinking of others — often at senior levels in the organisation. Other potentially daunting tasks include coaxing an intransigent manager about the value of communicating, or persuading an overly enthusiastic customer that the video he/she has set his/her heart on may not be the best solution to his/her communication needs. So how can you tackle these situations while maintaining strong relationships?

- Rule number one: use the business knowledge you have gained from spending time with your customers. If you link a challenge to a business objective — for your customer or the broader business — you are much more likely to succeed. By being a generalist rather than a specialist, you will be better able to identify with your customers, identify potential issues, and position your point of view from the perspective that it is the best way of achieving a business objective. Being seen as a help rather than a hindrance goes a long way in winning people over!

- Remember — one of the most important parts of your role is to see a situation from a range of perspectives. This is where you can really add value to customers, who may well be focusing on the project they have to deliver without linking it to other things that are happening in the business. Help them to think through the implications of yesterday's announcement of record profits by your plc on the communication they must make on capping overtime payments. Encourage them to get into the mindset of the people they will be communicating with. What factors will influence how people receive the communication? This is challenging your customers' thinking — in order to achieve the best outcome for them and for the business.

- Use challenge to protect the credibility of your customers. One communication manager interviewed recalled a major change planned for her organisation. She wrote a series of questions — covering all issues staff were likely to be concerned about. She passed these to the project team to answer. Where she perceived that the responses provided were inadequate she challenged the team on whether they were taking the right course of action using the principle that if you can't explain it, you shouldn't be doing it.

- Before challenging on any issue, do your homework. Analyse relevant data. Internal sources might include survey material or results from focus groups. External information could include press cuttings, information from trade associations or other relevant bodies on factors which could influence the issues under debate. If you don't have any facts to back up your point of view — go out and find some. Talk to other people and get their perspective. Arguments which are well thought through and based on facts rather than feelings are more likely to win the day — particularly in organisations with a strong data rational approach.

- Keep it simple. Choose key facts that support your argument and focus on those. You are more likely to gain understanding and commitment to your viewpoint.

- Always prepare in advance for meetings with customers — particularly where you are aiming to influence them. Make sure you can understand their perspective. What is important to them? What are their priorities? Their values? Doing this will go a long way to avoiding potential conflict. Some communication

practitioners use a simple checklist, such as:
— what do I want to achieve from this meeting?
— what is the benefit to the customer?
— why might they be resistant?
— what other priorities might they have?
— will they trust me? (if no: what can I do to build their trust?)

- Ensure that you have strong backers in the organisation. Win their support by initially focusing on supporting them and solving their communication needs, as described above. Your number one champion should be the CEO. You are his/her emissary — helping his/her vision of communication become a reality. This knowledge should ensure that blockages do not occur.

- Identify role models and use them effectively. Find opportunities for your communication stars to influence their peer group — and to explain how their approach to communication is helping them achieve their objectives. One organisation organised regular "communicators lunches" for line managers from different business areas following a communication training programme rolled out across the company. These both helped resolve a lateral communication issue identified by course participants, and provided a forum for sharing communication problems and learning from each other.

Responsibilities of the communication consultant vs. line manager

- Clarity of responsibility between the internal communication consultant and line manager is key both to ensuring the effectiveness of communication in the business and the sanity of the communication practitioner. It is neither practical nor appropriate for one person or unit to shoulder responsibility for the effectiveness of communication across a company. Responsibility for good communication lies with every manager in the organisation. He or she is critical to delivering messages, interpreting so they are relevant locally; listening and responding to queries and concerns, and generating local involvement and decision making. The communication practitioner is a facilitator, ensuring that processes, competencies and other communication tools are in place, monitoring their effectiveness against agreed standards and helping managers to be as effective as possible through advice, coaching, support and challenge.

The importance of the role of the line manager should never be underestimated. The Body Shop has a range of excellent — and innovative — communication media including print and video. It also has feedback mechanisms that go direct to the top of the organisation such as the Red Letter scheme — where a member of staff can write a suggestion or comment, send it to a director and be assured of a response within forty-eight hours. A voluntary communication network stretches across all departments and shops. The volunteers are provided with core information at a monthly meeting, and are responsible for ensuring that local areas hold regular communication meetings.

However, its first staff survey, held in 1995, showed that there was a need to increase the responsibility of line managers in order for communication to be seen to be more effective by staff. A programme to provide training, include communication in management competencies and increase the ownership of communication by manager, has now been started and is already bearing fruit.

- Ensure that the expectations of line managers — and the expectations they have of you — are clearly defined so that there is no ambiguity. Some communication departments draw up customer services charters, specifying the service they provide and the standards they are committed to achieving, and are measured against these. These will typically define the service a communication team is expected to deliver, its customers, and the standard to which the team is committed — in terms of timescales (eg: all phone calls will be responded to within 24 hours) and processes (eg: all customer requirements will be responded to by a written brief to be signed off by the customer before work is undertaken).

- Where an organisation is large enough to have a central communication unit plus satellite teams, it may be helpful to draw up a service level agreement to ensure clarity on each other's roles and the responsibilities each has.

- Different organisations are at different stages in ensuring that managers have full responsibility for communication. Some communication practitioners prepare communication plans in conjunction with their customers. Others provide customers with planning tools and train them in their use. The aim should be to encourage managers to see communication as a fundamental part of their ongoing decision making and planning process.

Paul Chapman, Director, Organisation Design and Development for National and Provincial Building Society, stresses that the role of the communication manager should be to ensure understanding of what the organisation is aiming to achieve and how, rather than to convert people. The task of gaining commitment rests with line managers. Attempts by a communication practitioner to win people over rather than presenting objective facts can result in loss of credibility (the Pravda syndrome). This makes the individual less effective in the organisation.

National and Provincial went through a radical change programme, re-engineering all its processes and rethinking roles and relationships across the company. The size of the communication team was reduced because the change was about releasing the potential of everyone in the organisation and giving them the skills and space to do things for themselves. The role of the communication team was initially to act as mentors, transferring their skills to others. Later, they focused on the logistics of the company's "Understanding Process" (see Strategy and Plans section in Chapter Three for details) and provided analysis of the wealth of feedback coming up through the organisation.

- The communication practitioner has a particular role with the senior management team in an organisation, drawing issues to their attention; and effectively holding up a mirror to show the team how they are perceived by others. To do this effectively, the communication person is described by the communication manager for Cellnet as "one enormous ear" — winning the trust of people across the company, and having highly developed listening skills.

Competent communicators

- To be effective communicators, line managers need strong communication skills, and to see communication as an integral part of their role rather than as an add-on. If your organisation uses management competencies, work with your HR department to ensure that communication is a fundamental part of the competency set used for selection and to identify future development needs. Increasingly, companies are measuring managers' ability against the desired competencies through 360 degree appraisal. This means asking an individual's manager, colleagues, internal customers and members of the individual's team to assess the person's ability to use a range of essential skills — and how often the skill is used in practice. Performance against the competencies is sometimes a major factor in agreeing the individual's annual pay increase.

- Make sure that effective development programmes are in place so that where specific skill gaps are identified, they can be filled. Have a range of delivery methods in place to meet different learning styles. Work with your training and development department to ensure that the solutions developed really meet the needs — and that they fit the culture of your organisation. Some companies going through a major culture change programme introduce blanket communication training to ensure a consistency of understanding of what is expected and why, and to start to equip people with the necessary tools. Others use a more targeted approach — identifying the specific skill gaps of individuals.

- Use employee surveys to monitor the effectiveness of the competency development programme. Publicise the progress that is being made and the help that is available.

Real life often means that line managers can be asked to discuss difficult or complex issues with their team before they have had the necessary communication skills training. The key to success here is to provide practical help first, and follow up with the long term development programme once the crisis has passed. With the issue still fresh in the organisation's mind, there will never be a better time to persuade your top team that investing in communication skills is worthwhile!

Parcelforce is a company that operates in a heavily unionised — and fiercely competitive — environment. It faced a potential crisis when changes in working practices to meet customer needs were rejected by union members in a ballot. Having made some changes to the original proposal, the company embarked on a major communication exercise. This placed a heavy emphasis on listening to people's individual concerns.

Every manager held local briefings, using communication material prepared by the centre. But they needed to be able to handle the specific issues raised by their teams — and to prevent the briefings from getting bogged down by debate on the detail.

A series of national and regional help desks were established, staffed by HR and supported by the communication team — who designed the process.

On receipt of a phone call from a manager, the help desks promised to provide an answer in general terms within 24 hours. The manager would then discuss the specific circumstances with their team. This increased the confidence of managers holding the briefings, while demonstrating that a listening approach was being taken.

Following a second ballot staff accepted the changes to working practices.

Communication skills are now part of an overall set of managerial competencies recently developed. Parcelforce's approach is to provide each manager with a structured document to use to identify his/her development needs. This is personal to him/her. It is shared only with a "mentor" (not part of their management line) with whom he/she will agree a personal development plan.

- To be effective communicators, managers need to understand the broader context in which they are operating — both externally and internally. Without this understanding, it is difficult for a manager to be able to put messages in their fullest context. It is important, for example, to have the necessary knowledge to be able to relate a change the team is facing to external pressures in the marketplace. Designing forums where groups of managers discuss issues on a regular basis with the senior management team is one way of broadening management thinking. Providing a press clippings service, inviting appropriate external speakers, or identifying opportunities for people to spend time with customers can also be valuable — particularly for operations which are not customer facing.

Making sure that managers have the necessary skills to communicate effectively is important, but it is not enough on its own. Managers must also see the value of communicating, so that they are motivated to make it part of their management style. When The Tetley Group introduced team meetings as one element of a communication strategy, time was spent with every function to understand their business issues and identify how the team meeting process could help them meet their objectives. This was time consuming — it took six months to complete the project in an organisation employing 2,000 people at that time. However, it was a worthwhile investment, building a foundation of real understanding by line managers of what communication could do for them, and ensuring that the team meeting process could be fine tuned to best meet business needs.

- It's not just line managers that have responsibilities. Some companies are now defining the responsibilities each member of staff has. The Body Shop Bill of Rights and Responsibilities spells out what all staff can expect from the company — and what the company expects in return. Communication is a strong underlying theme.

2 identifying customer needs

A range of tools can be used to identify the needs of specific customers and of the organisation. A vital element for success is to think through the implications and likely resource requirements of actioning the results before beginning the process, and ensuring the commitment for action is there. Raising expectations by involving a customer — whether a senior manager or the whole organisation — in identifying their needs, then failing to deliver for whatever reason, will lead to disillusionment.

Having initially identified needs, involve as many people as possible in the action planning process. This will both ensure ownership through the organisation, and the best results.

One-to-ones

- Rule number one: You need a deep understanding of the organisation, the environment in which it is operating, and the aims to which it aspires, before you can successfully identify needs. Chapter one gives tips from communication practitioners on how to increase general business understanding.

- If you are new to a business, start by visiting and talking with key customers. Use the time to understand their role; where they fit in the organisation and the contribution they are making. Prompt them to talk about their perception of key issues facing the business — and their area. Begin to identify what their communication needs might be.

- Some communication practitioners develop structured question lists to use as prompts for these discussions. Others prefer to let the discussion develop naturally. The choice comes down to personality and the culture of the organisation in which you are working.

- If you discover discrepancies between members of an organisation's top team about the company's purpose — don't be tempted to use communication to paper over the cracks so that others in the company don't see them. Where fundamental differences occur, it is essential that the team resolve them. Ideally, if they have the necessary skills, the team should go through the process of clarifying their direction themselves — to have total ownership of the outcome. Alternatively, use a facilitator (internal or external) who can design an appropriate process.

- Analyse what your customers say. They may find it hard to articulate what they want to achieve through communication and so tend to focus on immediate needs, such as processes to let people know what is happening across the organisation as a whole. Identify the most appropriate ways of meeting those needs and deliver them — but continue to monitor and focus on the deeper, cultural and behavioural issues which will form the bedrock of your communication strategy.

- Don't take statements about a desire to move to a more empowering or innovative management style at face value. Check out what is being put in place in other parts of the system to make them become a reality. For example, what changes are being made to the way managers manage and appraise their people?

Is there a genuine desire to change behaviour at the top of the organisation? If "empowerment" is simply an empty badge or slogan, putting communication processes in place to support it will be counterproductive for the company — and frustrating for you.

One communication manager reported that she quickly identified some immediate needs within weeks of joining her new company, and put a series of CEO letters and a newsletter in place. Within three months, through listening to people, she could see there was a conflict between the messages and the current behaviours displayed. She used this discrepancy as an opportunity to persuade the organisation of the value of a company audit.

Needs identification tools

- A number of tools exist to gather information and identify needs from the organisation as a whole. These include quantitative processes, typically the employee survey, which provide statistical data, helpful in identifying the extent of an issue. Qualitative processes are used to explore issues in more depth, understanding the reasons behind them. Many organisations use focus groups in this way. The most important thing for the communication practitioner is to have a range of adaptable tools in his/her toolkit — and not to be inflexible in their use. One person interviewed for the book reported that the process of gathering information in a previous organisation had been delayed for months — because of a disagreement in the team about whether qualitative, or quantitative, processes should be used first!

- Be pragmatic in your choice of tool for identifying

needs. If you simply want pointers for the way forward, you can use a qualitative tool such as focus groups. You should find that clear themes begin to develop within running just a few groups.

- When structuring any questionnaire, ensure that the questions you ask are directly relevant to your organisation (or the project) and its needs. Any audit should be directly linked to the company's strategic direction. Identify the behaviours and attitudes that are essential for success. Define key subject areas for the survey. Each of these should be areas where you have identified you want to take action to improve or which you know are issues for staff. Make sure the issues are both measurable and actionable. Don't overload the survey. Pick three or four key areas where you know the company will have the commitment and the resources to take action afterwards.

- Be sure that you have buy-in to the objectives of the survey before you start — from the top team, and other managers. Position the survey as something that will help them in achieving overall business objectives — an aid, not a threat. Ownership of the survey process by managers means that action is much more likely to follow the survey results.

- Take care to avoid too many people being involved in the design of the detail of a survey. It is important to get agreement to the objectives of the survey and the main areas to be covered. Other people getting involved in the precise wording of questions may prove to be less than helpful if internal politics start to get in the way of clarity.

- Once the draft survey is complete, imagine the answers. Will it tell you all you need to know ? Redraft as necessary.

- Following up a quantitative survey with focus groups can be a good way of overcoming the problem of people focusing on figures and statistics, rather than on real issues. Involve managers in focus groups — or in team discussions to get under the skin of the findings. Make sure that they have the necessary listening and facilitation skills first.

Focus groups can meet more than one objective. One communication manager described how she ran a series of focus groups to dig under the surface of issues identified through a quantitative survey. Each group was made up of a diagonal slice of the organisation — from different areas and levels. The groups were facilitated by directors. The structure of the groups helped overcome two phenomena identified in the survey. Directors were perceived as being distant. The company was also affected by the 'unknown plonker syndrome' — people from one area did not know the contributions that other areas were making, and therefore did not value them. Providing the opportunity to listen to one another began the process of breaking down barriers. The output of the groups was used to help build the communication strategy, meaning that people felt involved in the process.

Thinking through the process

- Whether embarking on a quantitative or qualitative survey, take time at the start to plan every part of the process. As a minimum you will need to:
  — identify the objectives of the survey
  — formulate the questions
  — pilot the questions: to make sure that people understand them
  — rewrite the questions (less important for a

qualitative survey where the facilitator can check understanding during the session)
— print the survey (for quantitative questionnaires)
— publicise the survey: explaining what is happening and why
— organise the logistics
— invite people to attend a session or
— for postal surveys: ensure you have an up-to-date list of staff/locations
  — carry out the survey
  — analyse the results
  — publicise the results
  — action the results
  — let people know the action you have taken.

• When inviting people to take part in the survey, ensure they understand why the survey is being carried out, how you will feed the results back to them, and what will happen as a result (i.e. what process will be followed to action the results). Also stress the steps that are being taken to ensure the confidentiality of their response.

• Confidentiality is important if you are to be sure of getting people's genuine views — except in companies with very high levels of openness and trust. Even if you have the skills to design a quantitative survey in-house, it is worth employing an external company to administer the survey and process the results. Publicise this, and stress the measures being taken to ensure individual confidentiality — for example, that the smallest size group whose views will be fed back to the company is ten, assuring anonimity.

• Publish the survey results. If you don't, people will assume that they are worse than they are.

• Regular quantitative questionnaires are a valuable

way of monitoring the success of change programmes. Make sure your survey includes a core of "benchmark" questions — directly linked to the key things you need to achieve as a business. But take care in using normative data, in other words direct comparisons with what other companies score for the same question. Many external organisations who offer a survey service will provide this data. But unless the other companies have been carefully selected because of the similarity of their purpose, strategies and competitive situation, the fact that they are achieving higher (or lower) scores than you may simply not be relevant.

- Most importantly, make sure that the organisation has thought through in advance what process it will put in place to action the findings — and that the necessary resource will be available. There is nothing more counterproductive than to ask people for their views then seemingly to ignore what they say.

Ensuring action and buy in

- It makes sense to structure surveys so that the results can be broken down and thus produce tailored reports for different areas of the business. This makes the results more meaningful and actionable. Spend time talking through the results from each specific area with the appropriate director or management team — as well as addressing the issues coming from the overall survey with the Board or Executive group.

- A company-wide survey and resultant company wide action plan can seem remote. Involving teams at a local level in action planning will help give the process validity in their eyes, and support one of the key principles of empowerment: that the most effective solutions come from within the organisation.

The BBC went through an intensive process to identify needs when starting on its major change programme in the early 1990s. A change management team was formulated — including senior representatives from internal communications, human resources, management development and the Chief Executive Officer.

The initial task was to hold one-to-ones with Board members, to research their views on the purpose of the organisation, its principal strategies and its brand — the essence, or values of the BBC.

Next, a rigorous survey was carried out, to gather perceptions of every aspect of the organisation. These ranged from the degree of understanding and commitment, to company goals, to management behaviour, to the effectiveness of current communication tools. This survey used an organisational model founded on the assumption that employee commitment and motivation produce enhanced performance. The model linked internal and external factors — a particularly important factor for the BBC.

Once the results of the survey had been received and an initial analysis had taken place to identify what the data showed, an intensive involvement programme began. This involved the top 250 managers in the corporation. The way in which this was carried out depended on the degree of interest and enthusiasm of individual managers. Formats ranged from formal presentations from the management group, to structured workshops involving business games and role playing.

Next, every manager was mandated to discuss the results with his or her team. They were provided with a suggested process and timetable, and given the task of identifying:

— up to six actions in their remit which would help their team achieve its objectives

— three actions at divisional level
— and one action at Board level which would help
   them do their jobs better.
   This was followed by a discussion at Board level
resulting in a commitment to improve in five areas.
Local initiatives were prominently publicised
through the internal media — to demonstrate what
people were able to achieve.

The Body Shop carried out their first social audit in
1994/95. This covered 10 key stakeholder groups,
including employees. The Ethical Audit department
— part of head office staff — developed the
methodology and carried out the audit, involving
other staff focus groups in identifying the issues to
be targeted, and at the piloting stage.
   Once the results were independently analysed, the
head of each corporate area was responsible for
developing their individual ideas on necessary
actions. These plans then went to the Management
Committee and the Main Board for final sign off.
After publication, staff had the opportunity to give
feedback on the audit results and give their input for
departmental action plans. They could do this either
by discussing local implications with others in their
own department or, if they chose, by looking at
company-wide issues at a series of voluntary
discussion groups.
   The output of this discussion was fed back to the
audit team who will report on progress towards
agreed action plans and next step commitments
made in the first statement. The continual cycle
begins again with a second audit in 1997.

- Establishing a working party is an alternative way of
  getting wider buy-in to the actions following a survey.

This group is likely to be cross-functional and represent a broad sweep of the organisation. This can be a valuable mechanism, ensuring that a range of perspectives and operational requirements are brought to bear when proposing ways forward. However, it is important that the group is made up of people who are going to be forward looking and focus on solutions, rather than to hold a post mortem on the results.

- When publicising the results of a survey or the action plans that follow, take care that communication is not treated as a stand alone feature. Actions being taken to improve communication should be shown to be integrated with other managerial or business improvements taking place.

- Having identified a potential solution to a particular tactical need, it can be helpful to pilot it. The Inland Revenue identified a number of communication issues from a staff survey and a follow up communication audit, including staff who were flooded with paper, and potential inconsistency of messages. One solution identified was to introduce a single regular management publication, summarising all the main issues which all staff needed to know about. This was then used for the basis of team discussions. The publication was introduced gradually across the Department, so that feedback from staff on its content and style could be incorporated at each stage to demonstrate a listening approach and to make sure the solution met employee needs.

- Having taken action as a result of a survey make sure people know what has been done, and that it was linked to what they said. Without prompting, people may not make the connection. Demonstrating that people's views have been taken on board is a great way of building trust.

The Royal Mail Employee Relations team in East Anglia initiated an internal communication campaign to highlight actions being taken following a national staff survey in Autumn 1995. The campaign, called "Plan It/Do It", aimed to involve teams in the action planning process. All teams had the overall results of the survey communicated to them, together with the results for their area. A series of communications followed, highlighting specific aspects of the survey and making recommendations on how to approach a people satisfaction plan. Teams were encouraged to mark the progress they were making, through displays on noticeboards, posters and in team meetings.

Royal Mail carries out surveys every six months. Responses for East Anglia in Spring 1996 improved by approximately one third — with 73% of non-managers and 89% of managers responding — the best response rate in the country.

3 developing communi-cation strategies and plans

Historically, the internal communication practitioner was a tactician, brought in towards the end of a project to agree how to communicate a business decision. Now the potential of the role has grown enormously — as has the contribution it can make towards the effectiveness of the organisation. This can only happen where communication is a fundamental part of the business planning process, built in from the start, with communication objectives directly linked to business objectives, and where listening is seen as being at least as important as giving information. This requires strategic skills — plus the pragmatism to turn strategy into action.

An integrated, strategic approach

- A company's communication strategy needs to be derived from and intrinsically linked to the overall business goals for the organisation. If there are elements of the communication strategy which do not link in to what the company is aiming to achieve overall, you should question why they are included.

- Communication is one of a company's key tools in moving from where it is now to where it wishes to be in the future. The communication strategy should therefore be directly linked to research findings. Andrew Lambert, managing director of People in Business, comments that very often this is not the case in practice — meaning that the strategy has a lower probability of success.

- A communication strategy will typically include:
  - communication objectives: linked to business goals
  - analysis of research: identifying priority areas for action
  - top level strategies: how improvements will be achieved. These could include:
  - processes for
    - delivering messages
    - feedback
    - involvement/empowerment
    - lateral communication
  - communication competencies: defining behaviours
  - key messages or themes
  - roles and responsibilities
  - communication standards
  - measures and measurement processes.

- The communication carousel outlines a simplified process linking communication strategies and plans to business need.

COMMUNICATION CAROUSEL

- It is important to get a range of viewpoints when developing a communication strategy. A number of companies set up a steering group to formulate the strategy and subsequently to monitor its implementation to ensure that it continues to meet business needs. In addition to internal communication professionals, these steering groups could typically include:
  - representatives from Human Resources and Organisational Development if appropriate
  - senior managers with a company-wide perspective: the deputy managing director, company secretary or head of business planning, for example
  - the head of public relations (unless PR and internal communication are integrated)
  - authoritative and highly respected line managers. The members of the group need to be committed to the value of communication. Don't include any sceptics at

the strategy formulation stage. Though the process could convert them, they will slow the group down and may increase the risk of wrong decisions being taken.

- An increasing number of organisations are integrating communication into every aspect of "the way they do business". The senior member of the communication team is part of meetings of the top team. Typically his or her remit is to represent the perspective of the employee at these meetings — with a brief to challenge other members of the team. He or she will therefore both influence the thinking of the group — ensuring that the implications of decisions taken are thought about at the outset — and will also ensure that decisions on what, how and why to communicate are intrinsic to every stage of the decision making process, and are built into the overall strategy — rather than being hurriedly considered once a final decision has been taken.

- Rather than having a communication strategy. The Body Shop builds communication into each strand of the company's main business strategies. This ensures that communication is an integral part of managing the business.

- Ensuring that members of the communication team join key strategy or project groups is an extension of this integrated approach. Again, this ensures communication considerations can be built in to every stage, while also having the benefit of broadening the business understanding and knowledge of the communication professionals, and giving an opportunity to contribute in other areas. Parcelforce take the opportunity to second junior members of the communication team fulltime onto business projects as a development opportunity.

Companies using the European Quality or "Business Excellence" Model have found this has helped to ensure that the importance of communication is recognised — and to position it appropriately as part of the management process. Post Office Counters described how, following adoption of the model, the need for a more integrated approach to communication was recognised, together with a structured, planned approach. Now, local heads of communication sit on each of the regional boards. A communication strategy was defined by the communication team at head office, with input from local communication heads. The strategy has been interpreted into an action plan, held electronically. All communication activity is fed into this, and progress against the plan is monitored on a regular basis.

- One way of making sure that communication becomes built in to "the way we do things around here" is to build it in to every meeting. A number of companies have a standard that every business meeting will include an agenda item to consider what should be communicated (to whom and how) as a result of the meeting.

- Avoid the temptation of acting on preconceived ideas when defining your communication strategy. Always test against the company's needs, and the information that research provides. Nicholas Wright, head of employee communication for Boots, believed that the corporate newspaper was surplus to requirements because of the range of business journals produced by each of the operating divisions and the changing nature of the organisation. However, research demonstrated that staff place high value on belonging to Boots as a parent company — and that the paper provides useful corporate adhesive, complementing the local vehicles. The strategy now adopted by Boots is evolutionary change, reflecting the culture of the organisation.

Using ears and mouths in proportion

- Every communication strategy — and each communication process used in a company — should have a feedback mechanism built in. Listening is probably the most important skill in communicating — and the one that is hardest to get right. Unless formal feedback systems are put in place, the combined knowledge of people in the organisation will be wasted. Real commercial advantage will come from understanding issues and concerns, and liberating ideas across the company, as well as encouraging managers to do the same at local levels. Identifying ways of releasing views and opinions, then harnessing them, is a key role for the internal communication professional.

- Two way communication can take different forms — consulting staff prior to a decision being taken to get their views; listening to their ideas and concerns; involving them in the decision making process. However, even one way communication, where staff are informed of a decision, requires built in listening, to check for understanding and to answer questions.

- Use feedback mechanisms to understand the issues that are of concern to staff — then build them into your rolling communication plan. People are unlikely to be prepared to listen to the subjects which the company is concerned about if the organisation is not prepared to reciprocate.

- Listening means you can assess what people heard you say. This may be very different to what you thought you said! We all interpret what we hear in the light of our own experience and expectations. Listening to how people react and respond to a message allows you to reinterpret and clarify as necessary.

- A listening approach doesn't just happen because the right processes are in place. Appropriate behaviours need to be there too. Ensure that company development programmes include listening and facilitation skills and encourage openness. Remember how hard it may be for some managers to listen to and accept challenge and criticism from individuals or in open forums, without reacting negatively or being defensive. Before starting such a programme, coaching to ensure an appropriate style is very important. It may make sense to resource this internally. Alternatively, this may be an area where outside help is useful, particularly when working with a senior management group, who might prefer to practise new behaviours with help and feedback from someone outside the organisation.

- Don't assume that the value of listening will be automatically understood. Do the necessary preparatory work to ensure that managers appreciate the need to take other perspectives on board. One communication manager explained how she took the time to feed back the results of the survey to individual members of the executive team, to ensure that they really understood not only what the results were showing but also that they role modelled the values of listening and facilitation. Then members of the team led mixed focus groups made up of people from across the company, to gain a greater understanding of their perspectives and to get input into how communication could be improved.

- A feedback system needs to include a process for actioning the information that comes back through it. Think this through and put it in place before you ask for feedback. Don't underestimate the amount of time it may take to analyse and action comments.

- Ensuring that action does follow the comments raised is crucial. One of the biggest demotivators is to ask what people think — then ignore what they say, or fob them off with bland responses. Encourage managers to put processes in place so that issues are followed through. If no action can be taken, ensure they explain why not — giving the quality of response they would want to receive. The director and general manager for Royal Mail Anglia has regular listening sessions. He incorporates any concerns into his personal development plan.

- Team briefing processes can be adapted to encourage team members to use part of team meetings to identify performance issues — then establish groups to examine problems and come up with recommendations, feeding back progress through the team meeting system.

National and Provincial Building Society (now merged with the Abbey National) went through a radical restructuring in the early 1990s. The result was a business organised along its processes. The company has four processes — Direction; Implementation Management; Implementation, and Understanding. The Understanding Process wraps around the other three, and is designed to ensure understanding of the company's direction and the contribution required from people, and to give everyone an active role in success.

Each member of staff ('team player' in N&P terminology) attends a team event once a fortnight. During this, the team first considers what has gone well or badly and notes any other issues. The focus is on what the team can learn from this. They also consider the aide memoire — a summary of key issues from the direction process — compiled by the top team. The meeting is all about the team taking responsibility for itself and its own success in achieving customer satisfaction. Where issues cannot be resolved by the team, they are referred to a point where action can be taken. Each issue is also noted and sent to a central point: the Opportunities to Improve Team. The responsibilities of this group include logging every issue raised on an "issueometer" and summarising the outputs of every team event into a document which is accessible to all. The issueometer provides an early warning of company-wide issues, allowing speedy action by the direction team (the top team).

Paul Chapman, Director, Organisation Development describes the company's approach to communication: " You have to win hearts and minds, so people understand what and why. Unless there is two way communication, you won't achieve genuine change. Communication is fundamental, to broadening people and to breaking down barriers."

The company developed its radical approach to managing the business by first taking the top team on a five day workshop, where issues were identified; approaches to tackling them agreed, and the next steps for communicating defined. Following this, a cascade of three day workshops covered the whole organisation. Managers' workshops followed a similar format to the Direction team and were hard hitting. Workshops for staff had a softer focus, to ensure staff understood the process, and that the direction team understood the issues staff were facing.

- Building discussion groups into the communication matrix can be a useful way of integrating feedback and developing understanding between people in different parts of an organisation. A number of organisations arrange sessions in which people have the opportunity to meet informally with a director or CEO to ask questions and discuss business issues. Added value can be gained where the director uses the opportunity to listen and encourage feedback.

- It can be helpful to provide invitees to discussion groups with a brief in advance. This should state the objectives of the session, and let people know what to expect, and what is expected of them. One communication manager also includes some background facts and figures on the company following feedback that staff would find this useful.

Inside and out — integrating plans

- In addition to deriving directly from a company's business strategy, the internal communication strategy also needs to be closely aligned to — or integrated with — the external communication strategy. It is vital to think of all stakeholder groups when planning a communication. Will the message you plan to give internally send shock waves externally — or vice versa. Many organisations have joint internal/external communication plans, so that the implications of a particular business initiative can be thought through from the perspective of all its audiences.

- Timing of major announcements has to be thought through carefully for different stakeholders. Most organisations try to ensure that their staff are the first group to hear important news. This may not be possible for publicly quoted companies where announcements with potential share price implications must be given to the stock exchange first. Here, most aim to give the information to staff simultaneously (generally using E-mail or other technological solutions). Explaining to staff why some information must be released firstly to the stock exchange is helpful.

Raising the standard high

- Once the communication strategy has been developed, it then needs to be articulated in a meaningful way. A number of companies do this by publishing communication standards. These are typically derived by identifying the gaps between where the company needs to be in its communication approach and style and where it is now, then devising standards which, when achieved will plug those gaps. Performance against the standards is then monitored on an ongoing basis.

Lloyds Bank went through a rigorous process before drawing up its communication standards. This started when grassroots feedback indicated that people were growing increasingly uncomfortable with the change being experienced.

First, the bank initiated research to understand the key issues and their root causes. Focus groups were held to gather people's feelings about the bank, and to identify what they would like to see happen to resolve those issues. Next, a quantitative survey was carried out, to validate the issues and identify how widespread they were.

The results were analysed and presented to the top team, who identified the top issues for attention.

Next, the bank initiated "the debate" in which everyone was invited to participate. Line managers presented the survey results and the priorities for action. They also described the process which would follow. Teams then developed sets of local actions, and made recommendations on what should happen nationally. These were fed to the internal communication team at the centre. They directed issues to different parts of the business for action as appropriate. They also developed the communication strategy — focusing on resolving the remaining issues.

The communication strategy gained the active endorsement of the management team. Next, it had to be communicated, but it was a weighty document. No one would read it all. So the communication team extracted the key areas which could be measured — and drafted the communication standards. But they wanted to make sure that the end result was relevant and accessible.

They initiated a further series of focus groups to test the draft standards and revised them in accordance with comments from staff. This process only finished when the majority view from the groups was that the standards were both understandable (ie not couched in management jargon) and measurable.

Now, progress against the standards is regularly monitored through research. The performance of individual managers against the standards is also assessed on an ongoing basis, and linked to the bank's performance management system.

Action planning

- A well thought through communication strategy provides a long term context for communication activities, ensuring that what happens supports the organisation's business objectives and goals. It also provides a framework and structure for activity. But a strategy is no good without action. It is important to have action plans which directly support the communication strategy, ensuring that progress is made and monitored.

- When defining a communication plan, think about different groups, and what needs to be achieved with each one. Awareness and understanding may be sufficient for parts of the organisation with some messages. It may be vital to have the active commitment of other groups. In general, where awareness alone is required, providing the information — and giving opportunities to ask questions and check understanding — will be enough. To gain commitment, a high level of involvement is essential. People buy in to what they feel they own.

- Companies differ in the support given to line managers to develop their own communication plans. Some communication professionals work with line managers and develop plans jointly with them. Others have evolved to the stage where they provide advice and guidance, but the line manager develops his or her own plan. To do this effectively, the manager needs a high level of understanding both of communication and of how to plan.

- BT has a very formalised planning system. Within the company, no business plan submitted for authorisation will be approved — or receive the necessary funding — unless it includes a communication plan.

- There will be times when you need to communicate quickly and there is no time to plan — other than on the back of the nearest envelope. Having clearly defined values, communication standards and key themes are useful here. They provide a useful checklist against which to measure your emergency communication — to ensure the maximum consistency.

- Even when you have time to plan, the chances are that things will change. So, is it useful to plan? Yes — because:
  - you can schedule your activities and organise your resources better
  - you can liaise with others to agree your expectations of them
  - the planning process encourages participants to think through the implications of what will be communicated as far as each stakeholder group is concerned. It therefore flushes out issues at the start
  - the plan articulates intentions and gives landmarks and a logical sequence of events. If these are shared, it is easier for the team to adapt and change with circumstances
  - developing a twelve to eighteen month integrated message plan, covering all the key messages and actions internally and externally, will flag up any potential clashes — the announcement of a reduction in benefits the week before a customer jamboree, for example. The plan can then be used to raise issues with senior managers, in order to influence and get counter-productive decisions or timings changed.

- Rather than including detailed messages in your strategy and plans, agree key themes. At a strategic level, these can prevent you from getting sidetracked by something that seems newsworthy — but doesn't have any strategic importance. At an action planning level, providing managers with key themes plus additional background information will give them a flexible framework to work within for maximum effect. Exceptions to this rule are where absolute consistency is a priority such as in major announcements.

Planning major change

- One of the times when the communication professional is very high profile is when planning for major change. It is important to be an integral part of the process — preferably from the start, so that you can influence people's thinking about how the whole change will be handled. You may be asked to lead a team to plan the communication. If so, construct the team carefully. Make sure you have got a wide range of viewpoints and experience. One communication manager in this position included a change champion and a resistor. She also made sure that a new person, and someone with long service who had "seen it all before", were involved. And she made sure that the team included a woman who had demonstrated a high level of intuitive understanding in the past.

- A key role for the communication person when planning a major change is to challenge. Think of all the questions anyone might ask. Put these to the change team. Get them to answer them. If the answers aren't credible — get them to think through the implications of that. An inability to answer a question could mean that insufficient information is available to take a decision — thus highlighting a key business issue.

Scenario planning is an important part of planning to communicate major change. One communication manager was part of a project team planning the relocation of manufacturing facilities. The announcement was due to be complicated by associated announcements regarding downsizing and capital investment. Final decisions on the shape of all the changes had not been made. The first task of the project team was to map out the communication objectives, messages and implications of each of the options under review. This process helped to flush out issues and so helped the decision making process.

- When communicating major change; make sure that the context is clear — explain why the change needs to happen. Use the time while the change is still being planned to paint a picture of the rationale for staff. This avoids a communication vacuum, and helps to prepare the way for the eventual communication by building understanding.

- It is a legal requirement to consult staff representatives in certain scenarios. For example, where redundancies affecting more than ten people are contemplated employers are required to consult individuals and employee representatives. Similar legislation requires consultation with employee representatives in takeovers. Work closely with your HR colleagues, who will need to be up-to-date with the legislation — and plan carefully.

- Whenever you communicate change, make sure that feedback channels are in place as early as possible. Understand people's concerns from the outset. That way, you can plan your communication from the perspective of the recipient.

The Royal Bank of Scotland has seen major change in a number of its operations. One particular challenge facing the bank in 1994 was the introduction of a new management structure. This involved every managerial job in the branch network changing. New salary and reward structures were brought in. New competencies were introduced. All managers had to apply for the new roles — under interview conditions that were new, too.

The new structure was brought in on a region by region basis. The communication team had a limited involvement in the initial introduction in Glasgow. Feedback from this pilot region demonstrated that staff had a number of unresolved concerns — and that early, improved communication would have helped to alleviate these in advance of the new structure going live.

The Bank was quick to learn. Before the next phase of introduction — in Manchester — the communication team ran a series of focus groups to identify what staff wanted in terms of communication about the new structure. Based on the output of these, a series of communications was planned.

Local newsletters were introduced to give staff background information about the changes. These included timetables for the introduction and for the communication opportunities leading up to it. The newsletters had a strong customer focus — reflecting a key objective that the changes should be "invisible" to customers, with no interruption to quality of service. Help lines were also set up to answer staff queries.

Next, all staff were invited to an evening roadshow where the rationale for the change was explained. This comprised a presentation from the regional manager, followed by a question and answer session led by the regional manager and change team members, and facilitated by a local member of staff. Team leaders had gathered some questions beforehand, and fed broader issues into the Q and A session while responding to local queries themselves.

Videos were distributed to staff for viewing at home. These focused on the different jobs on offer, and on the selection process. Job fairs were next. These gave staff an opportunity to discuss each role on an individual basis. The people who designed each role explained how and where the job fitted the whole. Then someone who had actually started doing the job explained what it was really like in practice! An HR representative explained the selection process after which there was a panel discussion. Attendees then had the chance to talk on a one-to-one basis.

The final phase was to advertise the jobs and start the selection process in earnest. The emphasis on communication continued. Prior to the cutover when the new roles were introduced, the Bank ran a communication programme called "employees as ambassadors". This comprised a combination of video and role play, stressing the importance of effective interactions with customers.

Measurement was used at each stage of the programme. Questionnaires were distributed after every event. Focus groups were run to identify hot topics and to monitor the grapevine and respond.

Peter Casebow, internal communication manager, comments: "The communication programme made sure that staff were clear about the change underway. Not just the details of the jobs and the process, but also about timescales — what would happen when. This went a long way to dispelling uncertainty. We also made sure that questions were answered at the earliest stage. And the bottom line was that we were able to continue to run the business successfully with this huge change underway internally — but with customers continuing to get a high quality service."

- It is important to think through what staff could be feeling and thinking in advance of communicating major change. Encourage line managers who will be handling the announcement to do the same. A checklist of questions for managers to use when thinking through their communication to staff could include:
  — will I still have a job?

— what will this mean to me?

— how is this going to affect my area?

— how much sense does this make for the business? People relate to change by thinking about the impact on themselves. Think the communication through from this perspective.

- Plan the detail of communicating the change, what has to happen and by when. Make sure there is a logical sequence in place, and that people know their responsibilities. Draw up a detailed timetable. This is particularly important prior to an announcement where one area of the business will be affected by the change and needs to be briefed first. Work backwards from "D-day" and think through each stage. "Prompt" the key players to ensure that everything is on track.

- During major change, there may be long periods when there is nothing new to say. Don't allow a communication vacuum to develop or it will fill with rumour and speculation. Give regular updates. Let people know what process is taking place; why it is not possible to communicate anything new at this stage — and when they can expect firm decisions. Most importantly, use your feedback channels to monitor rumours and respond to them quickly.

- One communication manager reported that the timing of a key change project was kept on track primarily because the date when the announcement was to be made had been announced to staff in advance. This proved to be a valuable tool in keeping sufficient momentum behind the planning process, so preventing a long delay in communicating from causing additional anxiety in the workforce.

- To be effective, and to provide the change team with all the support they will need — briefing packs, questions and answers, etc, you will need early access to all information. Going about the planning task in a structured and logical way will enable you to demonstrate why this is necessary.

- Where the date for a major announcement is fixed in advance, some organisations have found it useful to build in time for a rehearsal a few days before the event. Involving the senior managers who will communicate on the day reassures them — and allows time for fine-tuning. This needs to be weighed against potentially increasing the time between a decision and its announcement — so increasing the potential for the grapevine to distort it.

- Sometimes change is more evolutionary. Changing the culture of an organisation is a long term process — and requires understanding of the need for change to succeed. A number of case studies in this document illustrate how change can be achieved by involving people throughout the organisation — in a systematic way. Other solutions are more dramatic.

With cultural change, it is essential to get buy in as to why change is needed. The London Borough of Redbridge developed a radical way of freeing up discussion about deep seated communication and cultural issues. These included a long-standing tradition of secrecy and blame.

A cross-functional task force was set up to address communication as part of a radical review of the organisation. The group soon recognised that a communication strategy, focusing on information flows, would not be enough to get people to confront the behavioural issues which were impeding success. The task force decided to focus on a communication strategy which addressed the issue of how to encourage people to recognise the need for a changed culture.

Their solution was dramatic. They commissioned a playwright to research what working for the council was like, and specifically the perception people had about communication. He interviewed a range of people from across the organisation — from the Chief Executive downwards. He then wrote a play based on his research. The plot focused on a new middle manager working in a fictional hierarchical organisation. She took the organisation's statements about innovation and initiative at face value and tried to change things. The play looked at how she fared.

Initially, staff were invited to attend the play in cross-functional groups, then break into discussion groups to look at the issues arising from the action. Subsequently, the play was re-run and work teams encouraged to attend together. Following the completion of the drama, the actors re-enacted scenes. The audience were divided into groups each with control over one actor, and could stop the action at any time to comment on what they felt would really happen. This use of forum theatre enabled employees working closely together to voice views and opinions through a third party, the actors, which may otherwise have continued to be bottled up, straining work relationships and affecting performance.

Paul Williams, Chair of the task group which conceived the idea comments: "The play was very useful in freeing up discussion about the issues that people face because of the behaviour of others — and the consequences of that. Attendance was on a voluntary basis, with approximately 1,500 of the 8,000 strong workforce attending. A number of teams have now chosen to examine those cultural issues more deeply and work on resolving them — because the awareness and ownership is firmly in place."

Planning for urgent news

- Though you are unlikely to know when a situation requiring urgent communication is likely to arise, you can be prepared for it.

- Make sure you are clear on the processes you will use to communicate urgent news and that everyone understands what they are before the need to use them arises. Most organisations use E-mail as the medium for getting news out fast. In places where not all staff have access to E-mail, additional systems need to be set up. These could include designating staff in each area as communication representatives, with responsibility for printing a hard copy of the E-mail and putting it on notice boards. Alternatively, managers could be given responsibility for cascading the news to their teams. Make sure people know the timescale they are expected to adhere to.

- If you are relying on individuals within the organisation to play an active role in communicating urgent news, make sure there is a robust system of deputies in place in case people are out when the news breaks. Give clear instructions about what needs to be communicated, to whom, and by when.

- If you have to rely on faxes to distribute copies of briefings — don't underestimate how long it takes to fax several pages of information to various locations. The frustration of knowing that a briefing session is due to start in ten minutes but that you physically cannot get the information to all the briefers in time is an experience no communications person should ever have to go through!

- If you need to act fast — be flexible. Providing notices to the receptionist or to security to hand to people as they leave work can be a good way of reaching everyone if news breaks close to the end of their day. And people will appreciate the effort you have made — particularly if they are likely to see or hear a reference to what has happened through the media.

Companies with their own business TV systems are able to communicate a consistent message to all employees very quickly. Digital used its in-house video network when a new chief executive was appointed in the UK.

The new incumbent was an unknown quantity. He was joining from outside Digital and, even more significantly, from a rival company which was perceived to have a very different corporate culture. Speculation abounded.

Within twenty-four hours of his appointment, he was in the video studio. The objective of the recording was to give a flavour of the man — to present him to as many people as possible, to reassure employees and reduce the amount of uninformed speculation — straight away.

Within forty-eight hours of his appointment, the broadcast had been seen by fifty per cent of the employee population.

- Remember to follow up an urgent communication in the next regular team meeting or briefing. Encourage managers to use it as an opportunity to check that everyone has received and understood the information, or to give more detail as appropriate. Ask for questions and make sure they are answered.

Giving bad news

- Openness and honesty — to ensure the maximum levels of trust — are key factors when it comes to communicating bad news. Ensuring that line managers doing the communicating are equipped to manage the situation with maximum empathy is another vital ingredient.

- Managers need to be visible, supportive and available for their staff. They must listen and provide answers to questions where they can, and as quickly as they can. They need not be afraid to say they do not have the answer but that they will find out. This behaviour requires maturity and understanding. Think about the support your managers will require in advance of the bad news being announced, and put the necessary actions in place.

- Plan the communication of bad news from the perspective of the recipient.

- When planning the communication of bad news, make sure that the people directly affected know first — and that they are told face-to-face, so that they can ask questions and clarify their understanding. Having an effective communication plan, including a detailed timetable, is essential. Where people are personally affected; it may take time for the information to sink in, so provide additional opportunities for questions after the event.

- Make sure a robust feedback loop is in place, so that every question receives a response within the agreed timescale — even if the response is simply to explain why a full answer is not yet possible. Analysing the feedback to identify what the key issues are will help you as you go on to plan the next stage of the communication. Always make sure that staff concerns are responded to in the ongoing communication process.

- If the bad news is as a result of a business decision,

make sure that people understand the rationale. Previous work ensuring consistent themes, locked into the company's business direction, should help here. One company described how a whole segment of the organisation was told that a decision had been made to integrate their work into other business streams. Their jobs were therefore redundant. This decision was in line with previous messages given by the organisation about the need to improve competitiveness and service. Though obviously sad at the decision, the team worked with real pride to ensure that the transfer of work was done in the most professional way — because they understood why the decision had to be taken.

The Body Shop faced bad news in the Summer of 1994 when a press feature making a series of allegations about the company was heavily hyped on both sides of the Atlantic for a fortnight before publication. This had serious implications externally and sent share prices tumbling. Internally, the situation was potentially just as serious. The Body Shop is founded on very strong values — and the allegations were throwing doubt on how real these were. The potential for loss of trust was immense.

Transparency is one of the key principles for The Body Shop. The company ensured that all press clippings reporting the allegations were made available to staff on a daily basis. This ensured that people were aware of the accusations that were being made. Then they rebutted what was being said. A combination of media was used. This included bringing managers together to brief them and respond to their questions, then providing them with briefing packs to use with their people. Staff could phone a hot line to hear a recording of what had been said and the response. Notices and cartoons were stuck on the backs of toilet doors! These helped simplify some of the complex issues under the microscope.

Prompt action, and communicating with people fairly and honestly ensured that respect for the company was maintained while the allegations were still in circulation. The actual article, once published, proved to be far less sensational than the press speculation had suggested and the share price rose again.

Keeping it consistent: actions and words

- A key role for the communication professional is to ensure that messages across the company are consistent — and that they can be seen in a broad context so that the rationale for whatever is being said or done is clear.

- One technique used by a number of companies is to have a process whereby all messages for company-wide distribution must be "cleared" through the communications unit. This allows an opportunity to check for consistency of message, tone, style etc.

- Abstracting key themes from the company's business strategy, and checking every communication against them for consistency, will ensure a minimum of communication "clutter".

- Consistency comes from action — far more than words. Our beliefs are formed by what we see people doing rather than through what they say to us. Consistency between what a company says, and the behaviours it displays, is vital to build trust and avoid a loss of credibility. Everyone has seen the company where the values statement has been put up on the wall — and that's as far as it ever gets.

- Consistency in behaviour is far more likely if people have a sense of ownership for it and understand why it is important. Many companies use a workshop approach, bringing people together to look at the challenges ahead and what will be needed to address them. This gets "buy in" to the agreed behaviours.

Lombard Personal Finance have six core messages. These are an articulation of the company's values. John Morgan, managing director, comments: "Communication is a lifetime pursuit that can so easily be put back in a company, for example by changes in people. The values are therefore most important. They are what provide consistency."

The values were initially agreed by the Board, and disseminated through the company. Every action that the company takes comes from these six strands. The messages which have been developed from the values act as a yardstick against which all communication is tested for consistency.

John comments: "Success comes from using simple messages, and repeating them over and over, until everyone in the organisation can explain exactly what Lombard is all about. All our people should see themselves as stakeholders in the company. That means they have a right to know about the company, and how their job fits with the overall strategy. We need an agile company, with everyone sharing the success and the rewards, and understanding the need to change. You can't get that without looking at communication strategically.

"Improving communication — so that the recipient sees it as having improved — is a ten year process. Managers need to overcome the old mindset that information is power. That means leadership from the top, demonstrating the importance of discussing issues with people regularly, and honestly. It means having formal communication processes, and ensuring that every business strategy has a communication plan built in. It means educating managers to understand the value of open communication. And it means being prepared to use management processes if people do not behave in accordance with the values."

- Most communication professionals interviewed for the book advised a softly softly approach to communicating values. It's important to avoid them becoming management speak — with people being sent a personal copy but nothing changing. Instead, the company needs to put effort into building the behaviours espoused in the values into the way it runs its business — its processes and its training.

When Unipart was privatised in 1987, the new group of companies adopted a "stakeholder philosophy" as its set of core beliefs. The company set out to show how longterm, shared destiny relationships with its five key stakeholder audiences — customers, employees, shareholders, suppliers and communities in which the company does business — would provide a better business model for enduring success. The stakeholder philosophy suggests that in taking business decisions, the company should consider the impact on all stakeholders.

This has been demonstrated in actions as well as words. Employees enjoy a strong say in the running of the company through programmes like Our Contribution Counts Circles, a team building problem solving approach. They have their own 'university', the Unipart U, which promotes continuous learning in the workplace, an employee health and fitness centre called The Lean Machine, and an opportunity to have a financial share in the company through an employee share scheme.

In 1993, Unipart joined 25 other UK companies in a project launched by the Royal Society for the Arts. The RSA Tomorrow's Company Inquiry set out to study how UK businesses could compete in the new global marketplace. The results, published after two years of intense study and debate, stated that businesses will have greater opportunities for success if they can demonstrate an "inclusive approach" in which the needs of all stakeholders are considered and acted upon.

Initially, Unipart celebrated the publication through briefing meetings, supported by a special documentary produced as part of the company's in-house news video programme. Then, six months later, the company was given a unique opportunity to demonstrate how the stakeholder philosophy had been put into action. His Royal Highness, the Duke of Edinburgh, who is president of the RSA, asked to visit the company, to see how Unipart could demonstrate its beliefs in a stakeholder approach.

Rather than inviting His Royal Highness to a select meeting of senior managers, the company staged an event called Unipart Expo. This spanned nearly every aspect of Unipart's business, with audiences from all its stakeholder groups involved. The concept was to take His Royal Highness on tour through the Tomorrow's Company report, and illustrate it with real people who had done extraordinary things. This tour included presentations, an employee "birthday party", a tented village of stands hosted by community organisations, and a barbecue lunch for 2,000 people.

The aim of the event was to communicate some very complex ideas about trust and long term relationships with employees and other stakeholders — by showing how ideas had been put into action. In addition to involving the maximum number of staff in the event, a four page publication was distributed the following day. This was followed by a special documentary edition of the company video, Grapevine, entitled "Ideas into Action".

Frank Nigriello, group communications director for Unipart, comments: "Unipart Expo taught us a great deal about communicating complex subjects to a large number of people. I can't imagine that anyone could have left the event without being impressed by the power of the stakeholder philosophy and the spirit which people at all levels in the company have demonstrated in turning these ideas into a reality."

- Where managers are assessed against competencies, the appraisal process should reinforce the required behaviours. Monitoring mechanisms — such as feedback systems and company audits — can pinpoint any widespread issues and allow an analysis of why inconsistency is occurring.

Celebrate success where people are making progress towards living the company's values. Cellnet has a communication programme in place to remind staff of what they are doing to make the values live. Avenues for doing this include displays, news sheets, and opportunities for staff to share what they have achieved with directors. Other activities have included a charity ball and a family "away day" at a theme park. A people panel — made up of key players from around the business provides a sounding board for new ideas and initiatives. A "quality of working life" survey monitors progress.

- Context is as important as consistency. When a group of people has been immersed in a project, it is easy to forget that others do not have the same level of understanding. One of the roles of the communication professional is to help build bridges and make links.

This may be through representing the other staff to the team — asking the questions that others would ask —to demonstrate the need to give the wider picture. Or it may be through using communication media to show the links between what is happening in the outside world and the company's strategies and actions.

4 evaluating effective- ness

In a busy business, there is always the temptation to move on to the next priority as soon as the previous one has been actioned. Unless evaluation takes place, it is not possible to assess accurately the contribution that has been made towards achieving business results, to plan the next stage efficiently, or to learn and to improve.

Effective evaluation requires clear, measurable objectives, a robust data gathering process to build a picture of what change has occurred as a result of a set of actions, and the commitment to put learning points into action. Tools such as surveys and focus groups are used both to evaluate effectiveness and to identify future needs. A number of the examples in Chapter Two are therefore also relevant to evaluation.

Objective Evaluation

- Evaluation is only possible where clear objectives exist. Each communication strategy and plan should specify — in measurable terms — what it aims to achieve.

- Having clear links between business and communication objectives, and ensuring that the communication objectives are measurable, will help to make sure that the value of communication is recognised.

- There are various levels of evaluating the effectiveness of communication:
  - have people received the communication: are the channels effective? how good are managers' communication skills?
  - have people understood it?
  - have they internalised it — in other words, will they act differently as a result?
  - is what is being communicated through actions and words consistent?
  - what is the quality of two-way communication? are comments and ideas acted on or ignored?

- Make sure you are clear on what each of your communication processes are there to deliver. Are they there to consult? to motivate? to inform? to train? to gather feedback? to negotiate? Are they fulfilling their purpose? Clarity on the aim of each process will mean you can measure whether or not you are achieving success.

- Tools for measuring the effectiveness of communication include the qualitative — focus groups, telephone research, etc. — and quantitative written questionnaires. Surveys are often used both to understand how effective a programme has been, and to identify future needs. See the section in Chapter Two on needs identification tools for more detail.

- Make sure that every communications mechanism includes an integral feedback process to help monitor effectiveness. One company uses regular cross-functional discussion groups to build understanding of core strategies. After each session, group leaders are asked to fill in a feedback form listing unanswered questions, issues, plus any comments on the effectiveness of the communication. They also have the opportunity to attend a leaders' feedback session to give feedback direct — both about the subject, and the effectiveness of the process. This information is analysed by the communication team and amendments made on an ongoing basis.

- Use quantitative tools to measure the number of people who have received the communication. Alternatively, you may be able to build in ongoing monitoring of receipt into the communication process itself. This could be as simple as getting people to complete signing in sheets for major presentations. Electronic news-sheets may have a facility for checking the number of times a story has been accessed.

- Evaluating the extent to which a message has been understood is often easier to do through focus groups. Questions can be used to probe understanding gently through discussing the topic with the group — and to discover how they feel about it. Use of written questionnaires to do the same thing can make the person answering feel as though they are taking an exam!

- Evaluating the extent to which people have internalised the message is easier where there are specific behaviours which the company wants to encourage. Post Office Counters are diversifying the services that they offer their customers. A wide range of products now includes, for example, holiday insurance cover and an exchange service. A campaign was initiated to encourage staff to cross-sell — pro-actively suggesting other services to customers. The communication programme included an explanation of the rationale. Subsequently, regular customer research, carried out by MORI, was used to identify the extent to which such suggestions were being made.

- Measure people's perception of the fit between the messages they hear, and the behaviours and actions they see around them. Where there are discrepancies — put them high on the remedial action plan.

- Build in an evaluation stage at the end of every project incorporating a communication element — and make sure it happens! The pace of business life means that it is all too easy for this final stage to get missed or put on ice, so that valuable learning opportunities are missed. Think through how the learning one team has gained can be shared with others.

- If you have a communication steering group, use it as part of the evaluation process. The group can play an important role in assessing feedback and other data and making recommendations for improvement. Members can also gather feedback from colleagues on a formal or informal basis. Take care though that suggested improvements are owned on a broad basis by people who will need to implement them, rather than by a few key individuals.

- Using a range of evaluation tools will ensure the most robust understanding of effectiveness. BT combines an annual quantitative survey with qualitative techniques. The CARE survey covers a broad range of topics with core questions on communication asked on an annual basis to allow tracking. Focus groups, run by managers, are also regularly used. The company also employs an outside agency to carry out omnibus surveys — literally, stopping people on their way out of the building to ask questions about recent communications to test levels of recall and understanding.

A barometer group can be a good way of informally tracking effectiveness on an ongoing basis. Jane Mullins of Cable and Wireless Business Networks has

> identified a number of individuals across the
> business whom she regularly calls to gather reactions
> to communication. Carefully chosen to reflect a
> spread of experience and attitudes, they include both
> people who are champions of change, and others who
> are resistant to it.
>
> Where communication issues are raised in a
> particular part of the business, Jane asks a member
> of the group to probe further so that the root cause
> can be properly understood and addressed.

- Encourage people in the organisation to evaluate the
  effectiveness of communication for themselves, as part
  of the process of establishing ownership for
  communication where it belongs — with people
  throughout the business. The National and Provincial
  Building Society has team appraisals, where team
  members evaluate the effectiveness of all their
  processes, including communication.

- Self appraisal — combined with a 360 degree feedback
  process — can be a powerful mechanism for change.
  Where managers are asked to assess their own
  effectiveness at communicating against the
  effectiveness of others, a common result appears to be
  that each individual rates their own skills more highly
  than that of their colleagues! Once managers are made
  aware of this pattern, the need for change is
  understood.

- Evaluation needs to be followed by action. Make sure
  that you have processes in place to implement the
  learning points you have identified — so that you can
  create a virtuous circle of continuously improving
  communication.

5 getting the most from external consultants

The last few years have seen a great expansion in the number of consultancies offering their services within the internal communication and broader HR field. Used effectively, consultants can be an invaluable aid for the internal communicator yet used carelessly they can be a time consuming and costly mistake. To ensure that you are getting the most from consultants you use, consider the following key areas:

— what can they add?

— how can you work with them to get the best results?

What can they add?

- The main elements consultants can offer are:
  - knowledge and expertise: a thorough understanding of internal communication, current ideas and practice
  - experience as to what is being done in other sectors, markets and organisations
  - practical experience in developing processes and implementing their components

- Consultants can provide an independent viewpoint, offering a fresh eye on an issue with no organisational baggage. Using their experience, consultants are able to guide and help your thinking. Often their experience and understanding of other organisations and practices help consultants analyse your specific issues, circumstances, problems and requirements with greater objectivity. They can often predict the potential pitfalls of certain courses of action.

- Consultants are able to bring new skills and complement those existing internally. These skills can be employed only as required, obviating the need to employ extra staff to conduct a particular project. They can be replaced relatively easily to ensure freshness of approach, or if their skills no longer reflect the needs of the job in hand.

- In some circumstances consultants are useful in researching sensitive issues and presenting data in a less threatening way than if coming from internal sources.

- Consultants are often better placed than internal staff to challenge existing practices, beliefs or approaches and elicit a more constructive response.

Working with consultants

- Once you have decided that consultants do have a role to play in your particular initiative, it is important to select them well and decide the terms upon which you will do business with them. Some tips here are:
  — select an appropriate consultancy. In some cases a smaller local outfit may be more appropriate than a larger (and more expensive!) concern

- — ask for references from others for whom the consultants have worked. Ideally, chat with a few of the referees over the phone.
- — where possible, build the consultants into a combined internal/external project team. This may well be more cost effective and will help ensure a bespoke approach. It could also prevent others in your organisation from thinking that a body of expensive consultants are waltzing in, forcefitting one of their processes, and then waltzing out again, as some may be tempted to believe.
- — always make sure that consultants have a clear point of contact, capable of making decisions
- — do not be afraid to buy the occasional day's thinking from a consultant. They do not always have to work on long projects with you
- — where possible, work with consultants to transfer their skills to sustain a project in-house. This can save money and reinforce the feeling of ownership.

- As the project takes shape you can ensure that your relationship with a consultant is most productive if you:
  - — outline constraints and all relevant information straightaway, or as soon as they emerge
  - — give clear direction and welcome constructive feedback from the consultant as to its quality
  - — regularly monitor progress and expect updates, though try not to hector
  - — at the outset, agree upon the time required for a project and its costs as well as how either of these should be reviewed, if necessary.

bibliography

Communication skills: a practical handbook
Industrial Society, London, 1993   £16.95

The effective communicator   John Adair
Industrial Society, London   £9.95

Communications for managers: a practical handbook
Industrial Society, London, 1993   £8.95

Team briefing   Phil McGeough
Industrial Society, London, 1995   £12.95

Joint consultation   Roger Moores
Industrial Society, London, 1995   £12.95

Managing transitions   William Bridges
Nicholas Brealey, London, 1995   £9.99

Gower handbook of internal communication
Editor: Eileen Scholes
Gower, Aldershot, 1997   approx £65

Communication: why managers must do more
Researched by Dr Jon White; written and published by
Hedron Consulting Ltd, London   £45

Communication futures: technology
Smythe Dorward Lambert, London 1994 £75

The rise to power of the corporate communicator
Smythe Dorward Lambert, London, 1991 £25

The power of the open company
Smythe Dorward Lambert, London, 1991 £55

Corporate reputation: managing the new strategic asset
Smythe Dorward Lambert, London, 1993 £18.99

Communication futures: empowerment – any life left?
Smythe Dorward Lambert, London, 1996 £35

The communicating organisation
Michael Blakstad and Dr Aldwyn Cooper
IPD, London, 1995 £18.95

Consultancy: understanding the dynamics
South Bank University International Consulting
Conference, London, 1994

Process consultation Volumes 1 and 2
Ed Schein
Addison Wesley Publishing Company, Harlow, 1987

Articulate executive: orchestrating effective communication
Harvard Business School Press, Harvard USA, 1994

Communicating change
T.J. Larkin and Sandar Larkin
McGraw-Hill Inc, New York USA, 1994

Are managers getting the message?
Institute of Management, Corby, 1993 £30

How to be a great communicator: the complete guide to
mastering internal communication   David M. Martin
Institute of Management/Pitman, London, 1995   £15.99

Communicating corporate strategy: practical guide to
communication and corporate strategy   B. Quirke
McGraw-Hill, Maidenhead, 1996   £10.95

Strategic organisational communication   C. Conrad
Holt Rinehart and Wilson, USA, 1990   £34.91

Organisational communication for survival
V.P. Richmond and J.C. McCroskey
Prentice Hall, Hemel Hempstead, 1991   £30.50

Fundamentals of organisational communication
P. Shockley-Zalabak
Longman, Harlow, 1995   £46.80